EVACUEE

A REAL-LIFE
WORLD WAR II
STORY

Scholastic Children's Books
Euston House,
24 Eversholt Street
London, NW1 1DB, UK

A division of Scholastic Ltd
London ~ New York ~ Toronto ~ Sydney ~ Auckland
Mexico City ~ New Delhi ~ Hong Kong

First published in the UK by Scholastic Ltd, 2015
This edition published in the UK by Scholastic Ltd, 2019

Text copyright © Jan Pollard, 2015

ISBN 978 1407 9438 7

Printed and bound by CPI Group (UK) Ltd, Croydon, CR0 4YY

1 3 5 7 9 10 8 6 4 2

www.scholastic.co.uk

EVACUEE

A REAL-LIFE WORLD WAR II STORY

JAN POLLARD

SCHOLASTIC

CHAPTER ONE

September 1939

When the war with Germany started, I was staying with my grandmother in a little yachting town on the Essex coast called Brightlingsea. I went there every year for my summer holidays, sometimes with my younger sister, Hazel, but usually on my own.

My mother and father had a shop in London at Kensal Rise and we lived in the flat over the shop. My father's parents used to have a farm in Brightlingsea but the farm had been sold before I was born. My father became a shopkeeper and went to live in London. I used to wish we had always lived in Brightlingsea where we could swim in the sea and play on the sand and where one of my aunts had a hut, high up on stilts across the creek. When the tide came in, the water splashed almost up to the top of the steps to the hut – sometimes when we were having our tea. For a few pennies, one of the old sailors would ferry us back to the Hard, where we could climb out onto the slipway, even at high tide. It made a perfect day out, especially for us children.

I loved staying with my grandmother. She had a big house full of interesting things in her attic as my grandfather had been a sea captain: trunks full of old clothes in which we dressed up to act plays, and piles of old books. Apples from the orchard were stored in the attic between the beams and there was always a smell of apples in there, even when they had all been used up. There was a big garden with a stream trickling through it with a series of little waterfalls, and my cousins and I played in the stream, sailing a small wooden yacht. Sometimes we would see small eels, frogs and toads. We often fell in the stream, but fortunately it was only shallow and we just got wet – it wasn't a dangerous place.

I thought I would be going to Brightlingsea for every summer holiday during my childhood, but everything changed in 1939 when the war started and I would not see my grandmother, or Brightlingsea again, for another six years.

The year the war started, my mother, my sister Hazel, my baby brother Julian and I were all staying at Brightlingsea. We were just about to return to London where I was going to begin at the senior school, the

Convent of Jesus and Mary in Willesden, but my mother decided we had better stay where we were as London might be bombed. I didn't start school in Brightlingsea though. As nothing seemed to be happening my mother thought that at any time the war would be over and we would all be going home to London.

Nothing much happened at first. Just before the war started, the Government was worried that Germany might drop bombs containing poisonous gases. Everyone had to stick brown paper strips all around the edges of their windows to stop the poisonous gases getting into the houses. The paper strips were also criss-crossed over the windowpanes to stop the glass falling into the room if a bomb fell. Gas masks were given out, too, which we had to carry with us in a brown cardboard box whenever we went out. They were made of rubber and fitted over our heads with straps, with a mask sticking out at the front, to stop us breathing in poisonous gas. They had a horrible smell when you put them on and I hoped I would never have to use mine. My baby brother, Julian, had to be put in a zip-up cover with a clear window so you could see him. But he screamed so much every time he was put inside it my mother took him out after a few minutes.

Once everyone had their gas masks, there was a practice air-raid siren so everyone could try on their gas masks and find a safe place to sit in their house, because there were no bomb shelters then. We sat under the veranda in the back garden. After this practice air raid, we did not hear the siren for a long time. People started to call it a 'phoney war'.

On the 1st September 1939, a school from London came to Brightlingsea and the children were sent to stay with families in the town. The school was called George Green's School and the youngest children were eleven years old – the same age as me.

They were called *evacuees,* and had come from a part of London called Poplar, where the docks were situated. At the time, much of the food that Britain imported came through the docks in London and other big cities. If the Germans decided to bomb London they would target the docks, which meant that these children lived in a very dangerous place. So they had come to Brightlingsea with their teachers where they would be safe, or so it was thought at that time. The pupils' parents and families did not accompany them.

My mother got to know the headmaster's

wife, Mrs Humphreys, as she was staying in a house with her husband and children not that far from where my grandmother lived. Mother spoke to her about what to do with me if it became unsafe to return to London. She needed to go back to the shop where she helped my father and did not want to leave me with my grandmother for an unknown amount of time, especially as I had no school to go to. It was a problem for her. Mrs Humphreys assured her that if the war got worse and the children had to move to a safer place I would be allowed to join George Green's School and she would see that I was happily settled.

So my mother returned to London with Hazel and Julian while I remained with my grandmother in Brightlingsea. She thought that leaving three of us in Brightlingsea would be too much for my grandmother, especially as Hazel and Julian were so young. Everyone thought that the war would be over by Christmas, but it had hardly started.

The winter of 1939 into 1940 was very cold and the River Colne, which flowed into the sea at Brightlingsea froze over, as did the waterfalls in my grandmother's garden. I had never spent a winter holiday there and Brightlingsea was very quiet. You couldn't go on the beach and there was little to do. I had soon read all of my uncle's childhood books, which weren't very interesting for a girl.

To stop me from getting too bored, my grandmother taught me how to use the large treadle sewing machine which stood in her warm kitchen. She had been a seamstress and had taught tailoring before she married my grandfather and now she taught me how to stitch seams and to cut patterns out of brown paper. She made me a thick, warm navy winter coat and a navy gymslip and two blouses so I would be ready if I had to join George Green's School, as I did not have their uniform.

Spring 1940

At last the spring arrived and people began to look worried. France had fallen to the German army and at the end of May our troops had retreated to the beaches of Dunkirk, on the north coast of France. All the little boats around our coast set out to rescue them or to take them from the beaches to the big destroyers which were waiting in the deeper water to bring them back to England. The little boats from the Thames Estuary and the seaports along the south coast set off to rescue them. Over 338,000 soldiers were rescued this way. The sea had stayed calm all the time, which helped the little boats to bring the men to safety.

Now that France had surrendered to Germany, everyone was afraid the German army would invade Britain next and that would be the end of the war – the Germans would have won. It was also thought that it was too dangerous for all the children who had been evacuated to coastal towns in the south and the east of our country to stay there. The coast might be bombed or invaded. So it was decided that the evacuees should be moved to somewhere safer. This meant the children in George Green's School would be evacuated again and this time I would be going with them.

CHAPTER TWO

Evacuation
2nd June 1940

Before we were evacuated, my mother came for a few days to see me and brought a small, rather heavy leather case with her, for my clothes. She was a good knitter and had knitted me a navy cardigan to go with my school uniform.

She had been given a list of things to put in my case and these included a vest, a pair of knickers, two pairs of stockings and socks, six hankies, a blouse and a cardigan, a towel, soap, face flannel and a toothbrush and plimsolls. I would also need my gas mask, my identity card, a coat and my ration book.

Everyone in Britain was given a ration book by the government to make sure that food was shared out equally amongst people. The book listed foods such as cheese, eggs, meat and butter. We all had the same amount each week. Whenever we bought food, the shopkeepers would tick rationed items off in the book.

In another paper bag I would take a packet of sandwiches to eat on the journey, an apple and some barley sugar. Around my neck I would have a large label to say who I was. I expect I looked like a parcel when I was ready to set off.

The night before I left I was sent to bed early because I was joining the bus with the other children very early the next morning. It would be a long journey to a place of safety but nobody knew where that would be. I had a job to get to sleep as I felt very excited about this great adventure but I fell asleep eventually and got up as soon as my mother woke me the next morning.

All the pupils of George Green's School were gathered in Victoria Place where a bus was waiting to take them the few miles to Wivenhoe. From there, they would be boarding a steam train to take them to their destination. The pupils were very quiet and orderly as they boarded the bus. Nobody could tell my mother where we were going except that it would be across England, to a place of safety. Even the teachers did not know exactly where our journey would end.

I was only one of an enormous number of children to be evacuated. I later found out that on this day 47,000 children were evacuated from the coastal towns in 97 trains.

My mother joined a large group of

Brightlingsea people who had come to see the school leave. They were mainly from the families who had taken the children into their homes as their evacuees when they first came from London. Some had had the same evacuees for ten months and had become fond of them. In fact my mother was the only parent there as the other children's parents were back in London. Some of their parents had come by coach once a month to visit their children but now, although we didn't know where we were going, we knew that we would all be too far away for parents to visit us.

At the time, people did not like to show their emotions as much. I knew my mother would be worried about me as she said goodbye, but she would have expected me to be brave about it. My mother said, "Don't make a fuss," and she gave me a quick kiss on my cheek. "The war will soon be over and you will be back home in no time."

Perhaps she thought I would cry as she left but I was far too excited to feel like shedding any tears. I had been bored waiting to start school again and the other children looked as if, like me, they were looking forward to this great adventure too. I didn't know any of the children from George Green's School or their teachers, but I soon got to know the girl I sat next to. She was called Mary and was smaller than me and rather shy. I chatted away to Mary and we soon became good friends.

The train was getting up steam in the station waiting for us when we arrived at Wivenhoe and we were put into the carriages – the younger children together and the older pupils further up the train. The teachers sat amongst the pupils to keep order and to see all was well. I managed to sit next to Mary and felt very comfortable as I had someone to talk to.

Before we had travelled very far some of the boys opened their sandwiches and ate them but we were too excited to feel hungry. We had started off at seven o' clock from Brightlingsea, long before the shops had opened or anyone was around apart from the people who had come to see us off. I had not slept very well the night before due to the excitement of leaving and now it was catching up with me. Before long my eyes started to droop. Watching the scenery flash past the windows and the clickety clack of the train wheels as we sped along soon sent me to sleep, and I missed a large part of the journey.

The train didn't stop to let passengers on

or off but simply puffed on through all the stations, for hour after hour, until we arrived at a place called Hereford. The trains were changed here and we travelled on to a place called Moorhampton.

CHAPTER THREE

My first billet

When we got off the train, we were taken to the lawn in front of a large country house where some ladies stood behind a big trestle table and provided us with tea to drink and buns to eat. We felt very stiff after sitting for such a long time, but our journey was not quite over. Arrangements had been made to take us to houses, or evacuee's 'billets' as they were known, in the villages around this area. Some pupils went to Weobley, some to Norton Canon and Eardisland and Dilwyn.

Mary and I were sent to Dilwyn, a very pretty village with black and white cottages set around a village green. On the green stood an enormous white tent. We were taken into this tent and told to line up. Mary and I stood at the end of the line, holding hands and wondering what was going to happen to us. We didn't have long to wait.

A noisy group of ladies came into the tent and walked up and down looking at us – almost as if it was a cattle market and we were for sale. They chose children to go and live in their houses and took them away until there was only Mary and myself left. Finally, a young woman who was later than the others rushed into the tent and looked at Mary. I was suddenly afraid that I would be left on my own and I said to this woman, "We're together."

"Oh well," she said, "I expect I can manage both of you. You'd better come with me."

She led us across the village green to a

row of pretty cottages and we were taken inside one of them. There were a lot of small children in the kitchen who looked at us without speaking but the lady smiled at us and offered us tea and cake, which we ate gratefully.

We were shown the earth closet outside the back door in case we needed to go to the toilet. In the countryside, where there was no water or drainage connected, the toilet was in a small shed outside. It did not flush, and earth was used instead of water. Later, we were taken upstairs to where a double mattress was spread over the landing floor. This was where we were to sleep.

"I've put a rubber sheet over the mattress," said the lady, "because we've been told that evacuees wet the bed."

I was horrified. I had never wet the bed in my life, but of course I didn't know about

Mary and Mary said nothing. "I won't wet the bed," I said, very definitely.

The woman made no reply to that, she just pointed out the wash basin and jug in the corner, below which there was a potty on a shelf, should we need it during the night. "You'll wash yourselves there,' she said. "I hope you've got all you need."

When it was time for bed, Mary and I were sent upstairs first and settled down under the sheet. The small children in the family then came upstairs and walked silently past us and went into one of the bedrooms.

A light on the landing was left on so we could see our way around. As it grew dark there was a lot of laughter coming up from the room beneath which was the kitchen. I found I could see between the floorboards if I rolled to the edge of the mattress. A group of men were sitting round the kitchen table, drinking and laughing, filling their mugs from a large jug which they passed around. Mary was soon asleep, despite the noise, and I soon fell asleep too.

In the morning when I woke up Mary had already gone downstairs. I hurried to get dressed and joined her in the kitchen where we were given a big breakfast of bacon and eggs. Almost immediately a car drew up at the door and we were told to collect our belongings and get into the car as we were to be moved to another billet. If there was not enough room, children would be moved to another billet and there was very little room for all the people who lived in this cottage. There was no bed for us after all, just that mattress on the floor. The tiny bedrooms must have been very full with all the children in that family. But I think they were disappointed to lose us, because it meant that they wouldn't get our extra ration.

At that time when a family took in an evacuee they had their small rations to add to the family rations, which helped to make food go a little further, and they were also given a government allowance of ten shillings and sixpence to help with the expense of another mouth to feed. In 1940, butter, bacon, sugar, meat, fats and cheese were all rationed and later on even bread was on ration along with tea, biscuits, cereals, eggs, lard, milk and dried fruit. Only essential foodstuffs could be brought to our country by ship when we were at war because the ships could be sunk or bombed. There were no bananas for example until the war ended. Sometimes a few oranges became available – at the most twice or three times a year –

but these were only supposed to be for the younger children. I really missed bananas, as mashed bananas with a sprinkling of caster sugar and evaporated milk out of a tin was a favourite for teatime.

As the men went to fight, women took over their jobs including working on the land so we could still be fed. We even had to give in coupons to buy our clothes as the war went on.

Rationing

Here are some of the food items that were rationed during the war and in the years after the war. Amounts would vary from week to week, depending on what was available. Meals were cooked from scratch, so it was often difficult to make the rationed ingredients stretch far enough to feed everyone. Rationing was not lifted in Britain until 1954.

Food	Adult's ration per week
Butter	50 grams (2 ounces)
Bacon and ham	100 grams (4 ounces)
Sugar	225 grams (8 ounces)
Jam	450 grams (1 pound) every two months
Cheese	50 grams (2 ounces)
Eggs	One fresh egg
Milk	2 or 3 pints
Tea	50 grams (2 ounces)
Meat	to the value of 1 shilling and 2 pence. Sausages were not rationed.
Sweets	350 grams (12 ounces) every four weeks

CHAPTER FOUR

We were taken by taxi to Little Dilwyn which was only a short distance away and Mary was taken to a farmhouse. A young farmer and his wife lived there with a new baby. They had no other children. A lot of farm buildings stood round the farmyard, including a cow shed.

I was taken across the road to a pretty black and white cottage where I was welcomed by a young woman and her daughter. She was the wife of a farm labourer. They also had an older son, but I didn't see much of him.

The girl, who was about my age, took me round to show me the chickens and I helped her to collect the eggs. Later on we went down a lane to bring the cows in for milking. She seemed to think I had never seen cows before but although I never liked getting too close to cows I certainly had seen many in the fields around Brightlingsea. I told her that my father had once been a farmer but it was before I had been born and we now lived in London. She gave me a stick and showed me how to smack a cow on its rump to get it moving as we went along the lane but I kept well back – up close I found them quite frightening.

Over at the milking sheds Mary and I were shown how to milk a cow by hand and we were persuaded to try with a placid creature called Buttercup. I found the slippery feel of the cow's teats very uncomfortable and we only managed to persuade her to give a few drops of milk after our efforts. The farmer showed us how to go to the top of the cow's teat and then squeeze the teat as you pulled your hand down, but we were no good at doing this as our hands were too small compared to the farmer's big strong fingers. A long squirt of milk came into the bucket each time he showed us. Afterwards he dipped a cup into the pail and offered us a drink, but it tasted nothing like the milk from the bottle the milkman used to bring to our house. It was bubbly and warm and we didn't like it – it made me wonder how it turned into the milk we were used to drinking. Twice every day the farmer had to milk his cows by hand. It must have been really hard work.

After tea, I helped the lady of the house to dry the dishes. She asked me about my last home and I was only too pleased to chatter on about my grandmother's house and her lovely garden and the stream and the waterfalls. She stopped washing up and looked at me accusingly and told me I was the biggest liar she had ever met as she had been told that I came from Poplar with the other children and Poplar was a poor place – nobody lived in the place I had described. I was speechless at her outburst and for the first time I missed home and my mother. We only had a small back yard where we lived in London over the shop, and I wished I had described that to her instead of my grandmother's house. I had to remember that I was part of George Green's School now, from Poplar, so from then on I kept quiet.

Sometimes, when I wanted to be the same as everyone else, I would try to mimic the way they spoke. The children from Poplar spoke with what is known as a cockney accent, but I came from another part of London and my accent was different. The children often said I "spoke posh" just because I spoke with a north-west London accent, but I was not posh in any other way and their remarks hurt me. But try as I might, I couldn't speak with a cockney accent, so I had to give that up in the end.

My mother had packed a pencil, a pad of lined paper and some stamped addressed envelopes so I could keep in touch with her but the first postcard had been given to all the pupils and would be posted for them by the staff. Later, I went into the front room to write the stamped addressed postcard to send home so my mother would know I was all right. I was soon told the front room was kept for special occasions and I was expected to use the kitchen table. I had to learn fast that from now on things would be very different to what I was used to at home.

At bedtime I was expected to share the

daughter's bed with her. This surprised me but there was nowhere else for me to sleep and she made no objection.

The next day Mary and I walked to Dilwyn where the large tent on the green served as a classroom, but without any books or pencils or a blackboard we just played games and raced about on the grass.

At home-time we had no idea which way to go. The signposts had all been taken down in case the Germans invaded and the hedges were very high so we just plodded on. At a crossroads a farm worker, who was walking in the opposite direction, asked us where we were going to and when we told him he turned us round and sent us in the right direction. We reached Little Dilwyn late in the evening, utterly exhausted, with the people we were billeted with wondering if we had got lost.

After almost a week we were told we were moving again as there was no school nearby which could accommodate all the evacuees, so we packed up our small belongings and got onto yet another coach.

Chapter Five

Greytree
9th June 1940

We were taken to a market town in Herefordshire called Ross-on-Wye, which stands at the bend of the River Wye in a beautiful part of the countryside. This was to be our final destination.

We all gathered in front of Ross Grammar School and were taken to our new billets by ladies called 'billeting officers' who were in charge of finding homes for the evacuees. Mary and I went in a car with a billeting officer. When we reached the top of the steep road out of Ross towards a village called Brampton Abbotts, Mary was left at the last house in a housing estate while I was taken on a bit further along to Greytree, to a bungalow belonging to Mr and Mrs Warren.

There was a high hedge and a small gate leading into the front garden. As the billeting officer opened the gate a large white Staffordshire bull terrier rushed towards her barking loudly. I was not used to dogs and felt very alarmed but fortunately Mrs Warren and her two daughters were sitting under the apple tree with a picnic spread in front of them, waiting for their evacuee. They called the dog, Sue, who stopped barking, much to my relief.

I soon settled down with this family who made me feel very much at home. Dorothy was the elder daughter. She had left school and was out at work. Margaret, the younger daughter, was a pupil at Ross Grammar School. Margaret was three years older than me so we had a lot in common and became good friends.

As there were only three bedrooms in the bungalow I had to share Margaret's big bed, but as we got along so well it didn't seem to matter to either of us. Some mornings one of the dogs, Sue, would come into Margaret's bed and wriggle down under the sheets to the bottom of the bed. She was a friendly animal and soon accepted me as a member of the family although I felt uncomfortable sharing the bed with her. The Warrens' other white Staffordshire bull terrier was named Jill. She was much younger and not as friendly as Sue. Having never lived in a house with dogs before I found it difficult to get used to them at first, but eventually Sue accepted me as a part of the family and I lost my fear of her. I discovered she only barked at strangers and I became very fond of her.

In her bedroom, Margaret had a little wooden weather house on the mantelpiece. It was a source of constant amazement to me. When it was going to rain, a small lady emerged from a door holding an umbrella and when it was going to be a fine day a man appeared. I could never understand how these wooden figures could work out what the weather was going to be every day when the temperature in her bedroom only changed with the seasons, but they were always right.

Most of the household activities took place around the large kitchen table and the front room was only used for special occasions when a fire was lit in the grate. There was a piano in the front room and my mother arranged for me to continue my piano lessons with a lady in Ross on Saturday mornings. Margaret played the piano as well and sometimes we played easy duets together.

There was a range in the kitchen with a fire and once a week I bathed in front of this fire in a tin bath which was brought in for the occasion. At home in London, we had a bathroom with a geyser for hot water. The geyser was a small gas tank attached to the wall over the bath. When the gas burners were lit, they would heat just enough water for a bath. In Greytree the water had to be warmed on the kitchen range. It was a bit of a performance for Mrs Warren but it was a cosy place, bathing in front of the fire and I always enjoyed it, as the fire in the range was kept going most of the time for cooking purposes.

Outside in the garden, by the back door, there was a shed containing the lavatory. It did not flush. Instead it had a bucket underneath the seat that had to be emptied and disinfected. I don't know who had that horrible job!

The garden was long with a pigsty at the end, where Mr Warren's large pig lived. I was quite fond of the pig and used to collect sticky weeds from the hedgerows on my way home from school to feed him while I scratched his back.

One Saturday I heard a terrible squealing coming from the back lane and went down the path to investigate. To my horror the poor pig was being slaughtered in the lane and I was shouted at to get indoors. Mrs Warren explained that this happened every year – a pig was fattened up to become a source of meat for the family. The butcher had a half of each pig and Mrs Warren salted down the other half in the pantry. Meat was on ration and we ate every part of the pig, including eating the dripping – fat that melted and dropped from the meat into the roasting pan. It was spread on bread and it was very tasty. Bread and dripping helped to fill us up if we were hungry, which was hardly ever as Mrs Warren always managed to keep us well fed.

Not all evacuees were as lucky as I was. Across the road from the Warrens' bungalow there was a big brick house. Two elderly ladies lived in this house with their very small pet dog, which they used to take for walks in a pram. Two of the senior boys from the George Green's School were billeted with these ladies who gave them money every day so they could go into the town and find a café where they could buy themselves a meal. The boys thought this was wonderful until one day the money, which came from the government allowance for evacuees, ran out. After that they went hungry until they reported the matter to one of the masters at school. Then they were moved to another billet, the old Chasedale Hotel where all the other senior boys were now placed.

There were no such problems for us, because Mrs Warren was very good at making the food ration stretch. Sometimes she would remove the thick creamy top of the milk from the bottles and put it into a small screw-top jar. She would shake the jar over and over during the day when she had a spare minute, until the cream turned into a lump of butter. Dorothy and Mr Warren took sandwiches to work, so this helped out with the very small butter ration we were allowed.

In the garden, there was a greenhouse in which tomatoes were grown to add to our diet. Mr Warren grew vegetables and sweet peas too. The flowers were picked for the front room because they had a beautiful scent. Margaret grew the flowers in the borders in the front garden – asters and Canterbury bells amongst others – and Dorothy mowed the lawn, pushing the mower up and down. There were no such things as electric mowers in those days.

I loved to go into town to watch Dorothy working as a cashier in the big grocery store at the top of the high street. She sat in a little wooden compartment waiting for the receipts of sale to come whizzing along wires in small tin containers. She then put the customers' change inside and whizzed the container back along the wires to the customer. It was fascinating to watch.

Dorothy had a friend, George, who worked in the shop until he was called up to fight in the war. They kept in touch and would later marry. George went shooting at weekends and often brought two rabbits to the bungalow to be cooked in a stew if he had been successful. Mrs Warren's wild rabbit stew was delicious and made such a change from rationed food. She showed me how to skin a rabbit and afterwards gave me the skin to take to the butcher who paid me a few pence for each skin. I only had three pence each week for my pocket money so I was glad of a little extra. Rabbit fur was used to line coats and gloves and was very warm and soft.

Unlike our home in London there was no electricity in the bungalow. Every night an oil lamp was lit and put in the middle of the table. It gave a soft, mellow light but was not bright enough to write or read by and my homework often suffered as a consequence. The teachers at George Green's School were aware of these circumstances and took them into consideration when marking my work.

The Warrens did not have a wireless, as the radio was called then, so Mr Warren used to go to a neighbour's house to hear the news. He never discussed what he had heard in my presence so I was totally ignorant of the bombing in London or the dangers my family had to endure night after night. Sometimes pupils left school because their parents had been killed, but I had a letter every week from my mother so I knew they were still all right, although I worried about them. Mr Warren had a newspaper most days and this was left carefully folded until he came home to read it. I was never allowed to look at it. My life was happy and carefree not knowing what terrible things were going on in the world.

George Green's School shared the same premises as the Ross Grammar School, so it was very crowded. There was not enough room for all of us to be taught at the same time, so we sometimes spent half a day on the sports field playing hockey.

It was a long, tiring walk from the sports field to Greytree. There was a Japanese boy in my class who was also billeted in Greytree. He was very polite and, seeing me drag my feet up the steep road from the town, he would carry my satchel for me. I suffered from dropped arches in my feet, which is very painful. It made walking far a problem for me but there would have been no point in my complaining. Before the war started I had treatment in a London clinic and my shoes had been built up to help me to walk evenly, but that wasn't an option when I was an evacuee.

CHAPTER SIX

School days

Because of the overcrowding at school, on some weekdays we did not go to there for lessons but went on a Saturday instead. On the days when we weren't in school we visited historical sites, like Goodrich and Wilton Castles which were near Ross-on-Wye. It was a wonderful way to have a history lesson. We also visited abbeys, and farms to see the animals as well as going on nature walks to learn about wild flowers. It was much more exciting than sitting in a classroom!

Miss Harries, the domestic science teacher, taught us to cook using very limited ingredients available on ration. Eggs were hard to come by and we had to use powdered egg instead. Dehydrated egg was a bright yellow powder and was supposed to take the place of real eggs in cooking when making cakes and puddings, but they never tasted the same as when real eggs were used.

Mr Wagstaffe taught French and used to stamp our homework with his special stamp that said 'Félicitations de ton Professeur,' which means 'congratulations from your teacher,' even if our work had not been very good.

Mr Coates taught Art and gave me a great love of the subject, which has lasted all my life. He encouraged us to draw everything around us – everything from comfortable easy chairs to kitchen utensils. We had to use watered–down coloured ink called monochrome because the school had no paints and we could not use the dwindling stocks of watercolour paints used by the Ross pupils. Later, schools used tins of powder paints, which were mixed with water to make thick or thin colours as required. These were very effective and were used long after the war ended.

Mr Nicholls taught us singing in the Mission Hall, which was also used for PE, and midday meals, which were cooked by two of the master's wives. He used to turn the back of the piano towards us and stand up to play so he could look at us over the top as we sang so we would not misbehave. We sang English folk songs like *Bobbie Shaftoe* and *The British Grenadiers*. Often his wife, who had a beautiful soprano voice, would sing a new song first so we could learn it by hearing it.

Sometimes Mr Nicholls was a bit late for

our singing lesson in the Mission Hall and then we used to play around until he arrived. One day I was trying to balance on the back of a bench and fell off, banging my chin on the piano. I broke my two front teeth, but I didn't feel any pain as I only broke the tops off. However, I spent the whole lesson trying to sing with a mouthful of tiny splinters of teeth as I couldn't really tell Mr Nicholls what I'd been up to. I never looked the same afterwards and hoped no one would notice this change in my appearance!

The staff at George Green's School were like parents to us and cared for us in many ways apart from their teaching duties. The younger pupils were billeted out and lived with local families, in and around Ross, but the older boys lived in a hostel, which had been the Chasedale Hotel before the war, where they were looked after by Mr

Humphreys. Mr Wagstaffe and the teachers' wives lived in another hostel, Brookfield, with the older girls. The senior boys dug up part of the back garden at Chasedale in order to plant vegetables to help with the school meals. No spare ground was left for grass as every space was needed to grow food. But the teacher who was in charge of the gardening knew nothing about planting anything so they put in the onions upside down! They took a long time to grow, but they did in the end. They managed better with planting potatoes, and the boys provided most of the potatoes that we ate with our school dinners.

Miss Downing, the senior mistress, organized plays to be acted on the lawn at Chasedale.

The older pupils took part in Shakespearean plays with the help of the Ross Grammar

School pupils. I was in a play about Pandora's Box as a member of the chorus. Our costumes, which were simple tunics, were cut out of washed sacking material. In art class we printed a Greek Key pattern along the edges with potato prints. The boy who was to play the part of Narcissus disappeared at the dress rehearsal as soon as he saw the costume he was expected to wear, which looked like a knee length satin dress, and that proved to be the end of his acting career!

On the day of the performance, a wind-up record player placed on the lawn provided the background music. The dancing consisted of making shapes in groups to music – known then as Greek dancing. The shrubbery at the side of the lawn was used like the scenery in a theatre, and we all tripped off behind the bushes when our part had finished. The school staff and the other people in the audience seemed to enjoy the performance as much as the pupils taking part. It would have been nice if Mrs Warren had been invited to see Pandora's Box but of course they could not invite all the evacuees' foster parents and so I did not know anybody in the audience apart from members of the staff.

Time whizzed by at our temporary school and before I knew it, the Christmas holiday arrived. I was put on the train to travel to Paddington Station where, to my joy, my mother was waiting to collect me and take me home for Christmas.

CHAPTER SEVEN

Christmas 1940

The heavy bombing of London, which had happened every night for a long time and was called the Blitz, had slowed by the end of November 1940, which was probably why my parents thought it was safe for me to return home for Christmas, but they were very wrong.

As soon as Christmas was over the Germans bombed London, but this time it was even worse than before. The whole of the east end of London and the docks were all but destroyed. As soon as the air-raid siren sounded the Blitz began and the bombing continued all through the night. The upstairs flat, which my parents rented out, was empty because living on an upper floor meant you had to move to an outside air-raid shelter for safety at night, and nobody really wanted to do that. These shelters were called Anderson shelters and were pieces of corrugated iron bent over a hole dug into the ground. Inside you sat on a bench on either side of the shelter. It was damp and dark inside and very frightening as you listened to the aircraft overhead and to the bombs exploding around you. All you could do was hope that none would fall on your home, and if they did and your home was destroyed, then someone would come to find you, still safe in the shelter.

At our last house in Kensal Rise there had been an Anderson shelter in the garden but we had just moved to live in the flats over our father's business and there was nowhere for us to shelter on the night of the Blitz apart from the small cupboard under the stairs. It was used to store brushes and brooms, dusters and polish and boxes, which we sat on when the air raids started. It was stuffy but there was a small light bulb so we could see our surroundings, but the ceiling was very low. Somehow, because it had a little door, we felt safer there than under the table. Fortunately we only had to use it twice.

It was a terrible, terrifying night. We had no sleep for the noise of the bombs dropping. My mother was left alone with us because, as my father was an air-raid warden, he had to join the other wardens in the area, taking his stirrup pump and bucket of sand to put out incendiary bombs. An incendiary bomb caused fires and was smaller than the large bombs, which were dropped to destroy buildings. As we lived in north-west London we were more fortunate than the people who lived in the east end of the city, which had been targeted all night by the bombers.

We heard the noise of the planes returning to Germany in the early hours of the morning when my father came home. He called us upstairs to the empty flat to look out of the window where we could see a huge orange glow in the far distance, like an enormous bonfire or a firework display. As the smoke cleared we could see the silhouette of the dome of St Paul's Cathedral, which was still standing amongst the remains of other buildings. I found the sight of the top of St Paul's Cathedral surrounded by smoke and flames almost awe-inspiring. Until that moment I had been unaware of ever seeing it from our top flat as in the daytime it was too far away to be visible, but on this terrible night the whole world seemed to have caught alight and it stood out intermittently between the clouds of billowing smoke. I wondered what was going to happen to us – perhaps we would all be killed when the planes came back. After the peace and tranquillity of living in Ross for a while the world seemed to have come to an end and I did feel frightened for our future, even though I knew I would soon be returning to the safety of Ross-on-Wye. It was much too dangerous to be staying in London.

A few days later my parents told me that I would be returning to live with the Warren family who had taken me as their evacuee last year, but this time my sister, Hazel, would be coming with me, so she would become an evacuee too.

January 1941

Early in the New Year, on a bitterly cold January morning, my mother took us to Paddington station and put us on the train to Gloucester. There, we were to be met by someone from the railway station staff and put on the branch line to Ross-on-Wye where Mrs Warren would be meeting us. Apart from that we were all on our own.

This time we had a large expanding case with all our belongings packed inside as well as a hockey stick which had been my present that Christmas. My sister also carried her doll so we were laden with luggage.

At Didcot station the train broke down and we had to change trains, crossing over the railway line to another platform. The case was too heavy and cumbersome for us as we struggled to get it up the steps. By this time I was beginning to feel worried. What would happen to us if we missed this train or perhaps we got onto the wrong train? We didn't know anybody who we could ask to help us, and everyone else was rushing past us with their luggage so they didn't miss the train. They probably thought two young children belonged to some of the other passengers as we were very young to be travelling such a long way on our own. Fortunately the other passengers took pity on us and helped us to get the case on the next train, lifting it up onto the rack overhead, which we could never have done by ourselves.

Travelling alone was a little bit frightening for both of us although I tried to behave like the big sister who was in charge of the situation. If only my teachers had been there with us telling us what to do, but we were all on our own now.

Eventually we arrived at Gloucester station, where we were put on another train for Ross-on-Wye. During this last train journey Hazel often asked me, "Are we nearly there yet?"

Of course I had no idea if we were nearly there, as it had seemed such a long way to me as well. "We'll soon be there," I kept assuring her, "and then you will meet Mr and Mrs Warren and Dorothy and Margaret and the two dogs, Sue and Jill."

My sister had never lived in a house with dogs before and she was very apprehensive.

"Are they nice? The dogs, I mean," she asked.

"They bark quite a lot," I told her, "but only at people they don't know and they will soon get to know you. They live in the kitchen with Mrs Warren mostly and she is always there so you won't have to worry about anything."

CHAPTER EIGHT

Back in beautiful Ross-on-Wye

After our long train journey we eventually arrived at Ross-on-Wye and soon settled down living with the Warren family. Hazel shared Dorothy's bed, as there was nowhere else for her to sleep, except for the nights when Mr Warren was on duty at the telephone exchange when she shared Mrs Warren's big bed. It seemed quite natural to have my sister living with me at Ross. Mrs Warren never made too much fuss of either of us on purpose as she felt she could not take the place of our real mother. Even so, living with the Warrens was a very happy time for me because we were safe there from all the bombing in London, and the Warrens were a happy, contented family themselves.

As Hazel was too young to attend my school, she was sent to the village primary school at Brampton Abbotts. She had been used to a large primary school in London and now found herself in one long room with children of all ages from five to fifteen.

To reach Brampton Abbotts village you walked through the Dingle – a short cut. We loved this walk with its high bramble hedges and wild flowers, primroses in the spring and blackberries in the autumn, which we picked to be made into jam or put into blackberry and apple pies by Mrs Warren or Margaret, who helped with the cooking.

Sunday was the day for cooking in the kitchen. We were sometimes sent to church at Brampton Abbotts, probably to get us out of the way for a while. At the end of the

Dingle was a gate, which led into a cornfield with a path to the church and the school. Skylarks flew up from their nests in the corn as we walked along the path, singing above us, so high we could never see them.

My sister would hurry along this path on schooldays to catch up with the other children so she had company when going through the churchyard to the school playground. She found going through the churchyard on her own a bit scary.

The church at Brampton Abbotts was Church of England. We had been brought up as Methodists and were used to the Methodist services, especially when staying with our grandmother who was a devoted member of that church. Luckily, a husband and wife who sat behind us in church used to bend over to help us to find the place in the Prayer Book, and we were glad to see that many of the hymns were the same so we knew how to sing them.

We were often sent out on little errands to help Mr and Mrs Warren. We would go into the fields to collect sheep's wool caught on the barbed wire round the fences and put it into bags. Wool was valuable and was rationed on clothing coupons. Dorothy used to undo her jumpers and knit them up into different patterns to add some variety. It was called 'Make Do and Mend' and people made clothes out of all kinds of things, even old curtains. Everything was mended and clothes were passed down the family. Nothing was ever wasted. Sometimes, if parachutes were found to be faulty or packed incorrectly then the public was allowed to use the silk material for clothes, because it made lovely blouses and underwear. I bought some balls of camel's wool with my pocket money as it was not on ration. Dorothy taught me how to knit myself a pair of gloves which were soft and warm but a bit itchy!

We picked wild strawberries in the fields, which were very small and sweet, and even went pea picking in a local farmer's field, pulling the peapods off the vines and collecting them in buckets with other people. We were paid a little for the peas, after they had been weighed, and we were allowed to take some home with us in our bucket for Mrs Warren to use.

To help out with the food we would go to see Mrs Addis, a lady who lived close by, who had a long garden where she grew bushes of redcurrants. Hazel and I picked the sprays of currants for Mrs Warren to use in her cooking. Mrs Addis would make a batter for Welsh cakes, which she cooked on her range for us, dropping spoonfuls of the mixture onto the red-hot top of the range to cook in a few seconds. They were so delicious that we never minded going to pick the tiny, fiddly redcurrants.

Margaret told me that Mrs Addis had green fingers so everything she planted in her garden would grow. I had never heard that expression before so I used to look closely at Mrs Addis's fingers every time we saw her, but they never looked green to me. It took me ages before I found out it was just a saying.

CHAPTER NINE

Summer 1941

Sometimes in the summer we would have picnics beside the river with the family. A steep, unmade road went from Greytree to the railway line to Ross station. We crossed this line carefully by opening gates on either side and then we were by the river where the cows grazed. They went down to the water to drink or to stand and cool off when it was hot.

We used to catch sticklebacks in jam jars to take home with us and sometimes we paddled. People walked along the fields and fished in the river and others rowed in canoes. Beautiful bee orchids grew beside the riverbank, which we had never seen before, and we often picked daisies to make daisy-chain necklaces and crowns.

Some days I would go to the river with Mr Warren when he was fishing, and sit and read or learn something for my homework. It was a very peaceful place.

Mr Warren was a quiet person and very kind. He loved cricket and was a member of Worcester County Cricket Club. Margaret shared his love of the game and they would go to watch matches together.

We walked everywhere, especially when we had a school holiday and could explore the countryside around Ross. At the far end of the town was a high hill called The Chase where there was a path leading to the top. This was a long walk from Greytree, and was even further than the school sports field where I used to play hockey, but once we got to the top we could lie on the grass and watch the hawks circling above us until we got enough breath to walk back.

One day, we were walking up the path between the trees when we heard shooting below us and saw a red flag a little way ahead. When the shooting stopped we carried on quickly past the flag. Suddenly we heard a lot of men shouting and realized they were soldiers who were practising on a shooting range below and they were shouting at us! We had never seen soldiers there before and had no idea it might be dangerous.

We hurried on up to the top where we sat on the grass for some time until there was no more shooting to be heard. Then we made our way back. The soldiers had all gone by then and had taken the red flag

with them so we knew it was safe but we
never went for a walk up there again.

CHAPTER TEN

Autumn 1941

Dorothy was especially kind to us. Once, when Hazel had gone to bed, she knitted a coat and dress for Hazel's doll out of bits of spare wool so she had a surprise present for her birthday.

Mrs Warren taught us to play 'Patience', and Margaret also played card games with us which helped to while away the evenings as we had no other ways to entertain ourselves apart from reading. I think I must have read *Tarzan of the Apes* about a dozen times as this paperback was one of the few books the Warrens owned. We did not belong to a library like we did at home in London.

Dorothy used to buy a Woman's Weekly magazine, which got passed round the neighbours before Hazel was allowed to cut out the pictures she liked to stick in her scrapbook.

Dorothy used to take me to play table tennis with the air-raid wardens when they were off duty, and to see films at the cinema in the High Street. I remember we saw a black-and-white film called *The Great Dictator*. This was a film starring Charlie Chaplin and he pretended to fool around as if he were Hitler. As our country was at war with Hitler I didn't find Charlie Chaplin very funny but a lot of people watching laughed at his antics. There wasn't much to laugh about in those days for most people.

Miss Harris, the domestic science teacher at the school, took Hazel and me to see the new Walt Disney film *Pinocchio* which was showing at the cinema in Ross-on-Wye. It was the first film my sister had ever seen, and she burst into tears every time a bad character appeared. She cried so much that we both had to leave before the film was over. I was very disappointed when that happened as I had been looking forward to that special treat.

CHAPTER ELEVEN

December 1941

We still wrote home every Sunday and our mother wrote to us each week. Our father, who was a good artist, used to write a short adventure each week for my sister about a cow called Silky Moo, which he illustrated on the other side of the postcard.

We had been taught to say our prayers every night with a special request to keep our parents and Julian safe from the bombing and we certainly believed that would help. My mother never mentioned the war in her weekly letters, which gave us a false impression that all was well in Kensal Rise.

Of course this was not the case. I later

found out that because of the bombing many people had left London. Because of this, and rationing, many shops were struggling. There were fewer clothes to buy and nobody looked smartly dressed any more. Petrol rationing meant that people cycled whenever possible, so there were fewer cars on the roads. Everywhere people queued patiently for food, especially at the butchers. If there was an extra supply of unrationed meat or extra sausages the queues were longer than ever.

Some of the suburbs on the outskirts of the city had also been bombed and there were ruined buildings and piles of rubble along the streets. The parks nearly all had big silver barrage balloons tethered on ropes, floating up into the sky to stop the enemy planes from flying too low over the houses. It was sad for the people who had to stay.

At Christmas, my parents decided to come and stay with the Warrens for a few days so they could see us again and escape from the chaos in London. Hazel and I went to stay at a neighbour's house to make enough room for them. There were presents for everyone from my parents, who were very grateful to the Warrens for all their kindness to us.

My mother gave me a beautiful little watch with a black strap and a mother-of-pearl face, which delighted me as it was the first watch I had ever had, and it made me feel so grown-up. Sadly I did not have my present for long because I was foolish enough to wear it to school. During a break on the sports field while we were playing a hockey match I suddenly found myself surrounded by some bigger girls who demanded I hand over my watch to them. There was nobody near enough for me to appeal to for help and I was too terrified not to comply with their demands so I handed over my precious watch and never saw it again. I told the Warrens that I had lost it, which seemed better at the time than to tell the teachers, as I was too afraid of being bullied by the older girls if they ever found me on my own again.

Even with the upset of losing my beautiful watch, I was still so happy living with the Warren family that Christmas that I didn't feel homesick or have any wish to return to London with my parents when they left. Our mother was obviously missing us though, and I felt a bit sad for her.

CHAPTER TWELVE

1943–1944

The United States entered the war in 1941, after the bombing of Pearl Harbour. Shortly afterwards, in early 1942, the first American soldiers arrived in Britain. They were stationed at many bases all over the country, and in 1943, American soldiers were posted to the Ross-on-Wye area.

The American servicemen were made welcome by the local people. Dorothy got to know a Sergeant Duda who sometimes visited us in Greytree. He would bring gifts of food, like Californian tinned peaches. Tinned peaches with tinned evaporated milk was considered a great treat which everyone enjoyed because they had not been available for a long time.

Sergeant Duda's name sounded like "Doo Dah", so I used to tease Dorothy by singing the song *Camptown Races* in a quiet voice because the last line of the chorus goes, "doo, dah, doo, dah day."

At Christmas, all the children in the area were invited to a big tea party given by the American soldiers at the US base a few miles out of town, and afterwards we were given a large bar of chocolate each. We only had a very small ration of sweets weekly during the war, even if you could find them in a shop, so the big bar of chocolate was a great treat. We didn't eat our chocolate for weeks because it was something to be treasured and once it was gone we knew we would never have another one.

One weekend, my mother came on the train

to visit. I thought she had come just to see us, but she had a lot to discuss with Mrs Warren. It had been a year and a half since we had seen our parents and our mother looked tired and careworn despite her joy at seeing us after such a long time. I took her to the railway station to catch the train and wondered if we would ever be going home again. After we said goodbye, the walk back up the hill to Greytree on my own was a very sad one for me. I wondered if I would see my mother again. The war seemed never-ending and I knew that some of the evacuees had lost their parents in the bombing.

Soon after we found out why she had visited. My little brother, Julian, was going to join us in Greytree as an evacuee because the German bombers were bombing the Greater London area, including Kensal Rise.

My parents left our home each night and went to Uxbridge where they were safer staying with friends, and it would be easier for them if they did not have Julian with them, so he would come to stay with us until the bombing stopped.

My mother took him to Paddington station and he was looked after by a lady who belonged to the WVS. The Women's Voluntary Service were ladies who gave their time to helping people in need during the war. They collected clothes for people who had been bombed, helped with evacuees and made lots of sandwiches and cups of tea for people who had lost their homes. Mr Warren met Julian and the WVS lady at Gloucester Station.

Julian was a very good child and we were pleased to see him, but as he was too young to go to school, Mrs Warren would have to look after him until we came home from school in the afternoons. Mr Warren found an old wooden engine which his daughters had played with when they were children and my brother played with that.

Julian slept in a small bed in Dorothy's bedroom while my sister shared Dorothy's bed. It was a job fitting everyone in but somehow they managed.

Fortunately for Mrs Warren, who now had us all to look after, my brother soon returned home when the bombing raids became less frequent. It seemed quite natural for Julian to return home – almost as if he had been sent to have a little holiday. It was sometimes quite easy to forget that the war was happening at all. We thought the fighting would soon be over and we would be going home again to join him.

We were all very surprised one day when my father's sister, Dot, arrived for the weekend. We did not know Aunt Dot very well but I was given the job of taking her to see some of the countryside. I took her to see a famous beauty spot, Symonds Yat, where the river Wye ran through a deep gorge, and also to see the ruins of Tintern Abbey. I discovered she had come to get to know us as our parents had made her our legal guardian should anything happen to them. It was a frightening thought, as I did not want to go to live with this aunt if something happened to my parents. I did not want to think about the idea of my parents being killed in the bombing, nor did I want her to be in charge of looking after us, because I did not know her well at all.

CHAPTER THIRTEEN

Back to London

In the summer of 1944, my sister and I returned to London for what I thought was to be our summer holiday but it turned out that my parents had different ideas.

Although the V2 rockets were still falling regularly on the city, the worst bombing raids had almost stopped, so our parents decided to keep us at home and to send us both to the Convent of Jesus and Mary in Willesden.

My sister was old enough to go to secondary school by now, and if we had returned to Ross she would have had to continue at the village school in Brampton Abbotts until she was fifteen years old, unless the war ended before then, as George Green's School no longer had a secondary class for her to join.

Some years beforehand I had passed the entrance examination to the Convent, which meant that my sister could also join the school as a paying pupil so long as I was studying there too. If Hazel was staying in London, I would be staying as well. I was very sad as I was beginning to study for my examinations and now I had to start all over again in a school where I did not know anyone.

Life was difficult in London. Sometimes there was a horrible smog, like a thick yellow fog, caused by coal fires burning. It got into your throat, choking you, and you couldn't even see your hand in front of your face. It was so dirty everywhere, and we were not allowed to use more than five inches of water in our baths. Some people painted a line round the inside of their bath so they could see that they did not go over the limit. We even had to share the bath water – the smallest member of the family would have their bath first and the others would take their turn afterwards. I thought it was much nicer bathing in the tin bath in front of the fire at the Warren's house!

Everywhere, lawns and flowerbeds were dug up to plant vegetables so people could eat healthily. This was called 'Dig for Victory'. Iron railings around gardens and parks were all taken away to be melted down to use as the outer covering for shells and munitions.

At home, the top flat was being rented out and the couple who lived there shared the Morrison shelter in our living room with our parents when the air-raid siren sounded.

Morrison shelters had replaced Anderson shelters. They were made of steel with open steel mesh sides and were bolted to the floor of a room. The top was like a heavy table, and we used ours as a dining table and as a desk where we did our homework.

There wasn't room for me and my brother and sister in the Morrison shelter, so, because it was still dangerous in London, we had to sleep in a reinforced coal bunker outside the living-room window. My father had put sacks full of earth and covered with tar on the roof of the coal bunker to strengthen it. Inside, he had built two bunks, one for my sister and one for my brother. I slept on a mattress on the floor beside the bunks. Every night we went to bed in our own beds at exactly six o'clock and often fell asleep until the air-raid siren sounded, and then we moved into the coal bunker hoping we would be safer there if a bomb fell on our home.

An ack-ack gun went along the railway line every night shooting at the planes passing overhead. Kensal Rise station was close by our house and the gun made a terrible noise. We would be terrified until it had gone further up the line and we could hear it going into the distance.

We were so glad when the all clear sounded after the planes had flown back to Germany. The planes were Heinkel bombers, and their engines had a low, throbbing sound which we always recognized. Sometimes a returning German plane would shoot at the streets below and we would hear the bullets hitting the tarred roof above us, but we never came to any harm. Even so, I was made well aware that I was the eldest child and therefore responsible for my younger siblings, so I would try my hardest not to show them when I was feeling scared.

Once we knew it was safe we would go indoors to get dressed and have our breakfast. People came out from the underground stations where they had been sleeping and went back home or to work. The buses began to run again and we would catch a number six bus and head off to school. The bus took us to the top of the road that the Convent was on and then we walked from there.

Towards the end of the war, if an air raid had been on for a long time with no activity, people would try to carry on with their daily lives as best as possible, even though the all clear hadn't been given. This meant that buses would occasionally run during air raids. One lunch time, we were left in the cellar at school for some hours after the air raid siren had sounded. We normally went home during the lunch hour but on this occasion lunch was long since over and we were beginning to feel hungry.

Although the all clear had not sounded, very foolishly I suggested to my sister that, as we couldn't hear anything outside, we could hurry and try to catch a bus home. Fortunately a number six bus arrived just as we got to the bus stop but once we got to the top of the Rise, the drone of a doodlebug could be heard overhead. Doodlebugs were flying bombs that were first launched from the ground towards Britain in early June 1944. They were called doodlebugs or buzz bombs because of the odd sound they made. They kept going until they ran out of fuel before the sound stopped and then they fell to the ground and exploded. Nobody knew where they would fall out of the sky and they killed many people.

So when we all heard the dreaded drone overhead, the bus conductor tried to get us to go into the railway shelter with the other passengers but I pulled away. Taking my sister's hand, we ran as fast as we could the few yards to my father's shop. The front was open so we tore through and threw ourselves into the Morrison shelter in the living room where my parents were sheltering. The bomb fell onto the bus and destroyed it so we were very lucky. I never took a chance like that again.

Even without taking chances you never knew what was around the corner. One day, as I was sitting on the bus going home from school, it stopped at what had been the end of a road to let a small girl get off. The whole road had been demolished by a bomb and it was a terrible sight. The bus conductor got off and waited with the little girl until some people who were digging into the rubble ran up the road and collected her. For the rest of my journey home I wondered if the bomb had destroyed my home and if my family were safe, but happily my street was still intact.

Later on, when I passed my exams, I joined the Maria Grey High School for Girls at Brondesbury so I could study physics and chemistry, which were two subjects not taught at the Convent. I also took art as they had a good art department. The school wasn't far away on a bicycle, so I stopped going on the bus.

One night a V2 rocket demolished a wing of the High School building. When we arrived at school the next day the art class was sent to paint the damage. I decided I'd keep that painting forever as a reminder of the War.

After these frightening experiences in London I asked my mother if Hazel and I could return to the Warrens and Greytree at Ross-on-Wye, but Mother said that as I had left George Green's School and we were now pupils at the Convent and the High School it would not be a good idea. Mother felt sure the war would soon be over and I certainly hoped so. I would never feel safe living back in London until peace was declared.

CHAPTER FOURTEEN

The end of the war

On May 8th 1945, there was great rejoicing as the war was finally coming to an end. It was called VE Day and, in London, crowds of people gathered in front of Buckingham Palace to cheer the King and Queen. Princess Elizabeth and her sister, Princess Margaret, went outside to join the crowds and shout "We want the King" with everyone else before their father and mother came out onto the balcony to wave to everyone.

Peace was officially declared in August 1945 to much jubilation and dancing in the streets.

Some young evacuees had a difficult time,

but for me, those years when I lived at Ross-on-Wye were some of the happiest years of my life. We lived in a beautiful place and were cared for by a kind and loving family and we did not have to worry about bombs falling around us as we slept while we lived there. We were the lucky ones.

The Warrens became like our own family and we grew to love them as such. We have kept in touch with them all our lives and visited Mr and Mrs Warren and Margaret if we were on holiday near Ross. Margaret never married and when her parents died she had a bungalow built on land that used to be half of their long garden – the part where the pigsty was situated. Dorothy married George and had two sons, and when I married we spent holidays with them and our two daughters. Margaret used to come and stay with us for some of her holidays especially as her great school friend, Hilda, came to live in the next village to us in north-east Essex.

Mrs Warren never forgot my birthday and until the day she died she sent me a card and a little present just as if I was one of her daughters. Hazel and I still visit Ross and Ledbury, where Dorothy lives. Ross is a beautiful place and will always seem like a second home to us.

AUTHOR'S NOTE

I first wrote of my experiences as an evacuee as a special 90th birthday present for Dorothy – the eldest daughter of Mr and Mrs Warren, the people to whom I was sent as an evacuee all those years ago.

I had lots of old photographs which Dorothy had taken of me, and later of my sister and my little brother when they joined me as the bombing got worse in London, where my parents lived. So I added these photos to the birthday book to make it more interesting for Dorothy. Then I had the pages made into a proper book by a local printer to make the birthday present even more special.

Dorothy and her sister, Margaret, both

loved the book about all the places around Ross-on-Wye and the memories of the things we did together. So many people have enjoyed reading it that I have made it into a book that everyone can read and enjoy and also understand just what it was like to be sent away from your family not knowing where you were going or where you would end up, and find yourself living in a strange place with complete strangers without knowing if you would ever see your parents or your relations again.

I was lucky to live with such a kind family who over the years made me feel like a part of their family and whom I have gone on to visit regularly and will always think of as a part of my own family.

MR AND MRS WARREN WITH
JILL AND SUE THE DOGS.

MARGARET WITH JAN, HAZEL AND THE DOGS.

JAN, JULIAN AND HAZEL IN THE GARDEN.

JAN'S DRAWING OF BOMB DAMAGE AT HER SCHOOL.